COPING WITH

ADD/ADHD

(Attention Deficit Disorder/Attention
Deficit Hyperactivity Disorder)

Jaydene Morrison, M.S.

THE ROSEN PUBLISHING GROUP, INC./NEW YORK

Published in 1996 by The Rosen Publishing Group, Inc.
29 East 21st Street, New York, NY 10010

First Edition

Library of Congress Cataloging–in–Publication Data

Morrison, Jaydene.
    Coping with ADD/ADHD : attention deficit disorder/attention deficit hyperactivity disorder / Jaydene Morrison. — 1st ed.
        p.   cm.
    Includes bibliographical references and index.
    Summary: Identifies the syndrome of attention deficit disorder and discusses the appropriate treatment and counseling.
    ISBN 0-8239-2070-4
    1. Attention-deficit hyperactivity disorder—Juvenile literature.
[1. Attention-deficit hyperactivity disorder.]   I. Title.
RJ506.H9M665   1995
618.92'8589—dc20   95-41284
                                                              CIP
                                                              AC

Manufactured in the United States of America

*To my beautiful
and
precious granddaughter,
Blair Morrison.*

Acknowledgments

It is with deep appreciation that I acknowledge Carla Morrison for her proofreading and valuable suggestions on this book. Carla is a Library Media Specialist at Jarman Junior High School in the Mid-Del Public School System.

A special thank-you to my friends, my mother, Katy Walker, and especially my children, Mac, Lori, Jay, and Kerri Morrison, for their support and understanding during the writing of this book.

About the Author

Jaydene Morrison is a native-born Oklahoman of pioneer stock. Her great-grandfather was a country doctor who made the historical Cherokee Strip Run into Oklahoma in 1893. Holder of eight teaching certificates, she is a Nationally Certified School Psychologist, with a Master's Degree from Oklahoma State University plus over 60 hours of additional training from OSU and other universities. She is a Licensed Professional Counselor (LPC) and Licensed Marriage and Family Therapist (LMFT).

Jaydene's family consists of her two sons, Jay and Mac, and their wives Kerri and Lori. Blair Morrison is her delightful granddaughter.

Jaydene is presently enjoying the Hawaiian sunsets while working for the Department of Education in Hawaii.

Contents

CHAPTER 1

"Jason, Pay Attention!"

E veryone was always mad at Jason. For as long as he could remember, adults had yelled at him. "Jason, pay attention!" "Jason, quit it!" "Jason, how many times do I have to tell you?" "Jason, what's wrong with you?" How he hated to hear those words! He could hear them in his sleep. He had even come to hate his name.

His high school counselor, Ms. O'Hara, had first talked to him last year. In fact, Ms. O'Hara and Jason had talked a lot about his problems last year. She had said that his constantly being in trouble in school combined with his difficulty with grades might be the result of something called ADD. She wanted to have him tested at school and then have the test reviewed by a medical doctor, who could make a diagnosis. If ADD was diagnosed and shown to be affecting his ability to learn, he could receive special help at school.

Jason hadn't wanted Ms. O'Hara to talk to his parents last year. He knew they thought that he was lazy. He was sure they would just say he was making excuses for his grades if he told them what Ms. O'Hara said. But the new school year was almost here, and Jason dreaded going back to the usual struggles.

Jason went to the library to look up ADD. He told the librarian what he wanted. She explained that there were two terms—ADD and ADHD. ADD meant Attention Deficit Disorder. ADHD meant Attention Deficit Hyperactivity Disorder. People with either disorder had trouble paying attention and being impulsive. People with ADHD also had hyperactivity. The librarian said that 3 percent to 5 percent of school-age children were affected by one or the other.

She showed Jason a book called *A Parent's Guide* by Sam and Michael Goldstein. The book said that children with ADD/ADHD have difficulty:

- beginning activities
- keeping attention focused until the activity is complete
- focusing attention on more than one thing, such as watching a teacher and taking notes
- screening out distracting events in the environment
- thinking before they act
- weighing the consequences of their actions
- planning future actions
- following rules.

The result of this inattention and distractibility is poor or inconsistent performance in many situations. Impulsive, unthinking behavior often causes problems for the person who has ADD/ADHD.

Jason thought about how often he had not planned to get in trouble but it just happened. He never understood

how. He knew he was impulsive, but he didn't mean to
be.

The librarian came over, touched him on the shoulder,
and said, "Jason, everyone has gone home. We're ready
to close up for the night." Jason looked at his watch. He
couldn't believe he had been there for two hours. He,
Jason, who couldn't concentrate on anything for more
than ten minutes, had been reading at the library for two
hours.

When he arrived home, his mother angrily met him at
the door. "Where have you been? Your father and I were
ready to call the police. I've told you over and over to call
me if you're going to be late. When will you ever grow
up? Your father may have to take your car privileges away
again to help you remember."

Jason closed his ears to her voice, as he had for years.
He had learned not to reply. Saying anything only made
things worse. Today it was just more than he could handle.
He kept walking.

When reading about ADD/ADHD at the library, he had
begun to feel hopeful about his life. The book said that
the things that happened to him happened to many
people. He felt as if someone understood. His problems
couldn't be as bad as they seemed if other people had
them too. But his mother's nagging took some of that
hope away.

At dinner that night, Jason finally worked up enough
courage to ask his parents if Ms. O'Hara could come over
and talk to them about something. His father sighed, and
said, "Jason, this is typical. A week before school starts is
a little late to be discussing anything. Why didn't Ms.
O'Hara talk to us last spring?"

Jason didn't say anything. The room grew quiet.

His father finally said, "Oh, well. Have her come on

over. We may as well get this over with."

Ms. O'Hara came the next day and told Jason's parents that she suspected that he had ADD. She explained that the disorder could be the cause of Jason's inattention and impulsiveness. With help, Ms. O'Hara said, Jason could learn to manage his ADD.

After Ms. O'Hara left, Jason's mother said, "We never realized the struggles you were having. We thought you just weren't trying hard enough. Why didn't you talk to us before this?"

Jason replied, "I didn't think you would understand. And besides, you never seemed to listen."

Jason's father said, "You are the most important person in our lives. We want what's best for you. We didn't realize that your behavior could actually be a disorder. I think it would be a good idea to do some research. In the meantime, let's have the tests done at school. Then we'll see a doctor who has experience with ADD/ADHD kids. I want a careful evaluation done. If it turns out that you have this disorder, we'll all have to work together to cope with it. Your mother and I will work with you and with Ms. O'Hara and your teachers and the doctor. We'll look into all the ways that people manage ADD/ADHD successfully."

Jason started to feel hopeful again. It felt good to have his parents on his side. Maybe things would improve now.

CHAPTER 2

What Is ADD/ADHD?

Based on current research, most experts believe that ADD/ADHD is a neurobiological disorder. "Neurobiological" refers to the structure, chemistry, and function of parts of the brain. In people with ADD/ADHD, there may be imbalances or differences in the chemicals used by the brain to control activity, attention, motor skills, and some other aspects of behavior. One major study, by researchers at the National Institute for Mental Health, published (1990) in the *New England Journal of Medicine*, found that people with ADD/ADHD used energy at a different rate in parts of their brains than people without the disorder.

What could cause these differences? No single cause is known. Heredity seems to play a strong role. If you have ADD/ADHD, you may have inherited it from a parent. Problems during pregnancy or at birth may also play a part. ADD/ADHD has nothing to do with intelligence. And most specialists see no link with sugar, food additives, or inner-ear problems, all of which have been studied for possible connections. ADD/ADHD is a recognized diagnosis, both medically and legally. However, some doctors, psychologists, and others continue to debate whether it really is a disorder in its own right or a convenient way to describe a number of symptoms or problems. Researchers continue to look for definitive answers.

A Deficit in Attention

Everyone has trouble focusing attention sometimes. There can be many reasons you can't concentrate and listen. Perhaps you're upset about a relationship with someone. Or you're mad at your parents. Or you have exciting plans coming up and they're all you can think about. These distractions are temporary. Soon you find you can pay attention again.

But some people have had attention problems for as long as they can remember. They can seldom concentrate on the subject at hand for more than a few minutes. This can sometimes be a symptom of ADD.

Other people have long-term attention problems and are also hyperactive. This means they are too active. They can't sit still, but are always moving and fidgeting. These can be symptoms of Attention Deficit Hyperactive Disorder, or ADHD.

As many as 3 percent to 5 percent of school-age children may have ADD/ADHD. Both boys and girls are affected, but the diagnosis is made more often in boys. This could be in part because boys have hyperactivity symptoms more than girls do, which makes the symptoms more noticeable. Adults may think a teenager who has ADD symptoms without hyperactivity is unmotivated or depressed, and they may fail to notice the attention-related problems.

Overdiagnosis

While ADD/ADHD may not be recognized often enough in some cases, many doctors worry that it is inaccurately diagnosed much too often in young people. These children and teens are being incorrectly treated and medicated, and the real causes of their problems go unsolved.

Why is there overdiagnosis? Probably several factors combine to produce these mistakes. First, ADD/ADHD can be difficult to diagnose. There is no laboratory test for it, as the American Psychiatric Association's *Diagnostic and Statistical Manual of Mental Disorders* points out. It is not diagnosed by its cause, which is unknown, but by descriptions and evaluations of its symptoms. These are often the same as symptoms of other disorders, such as depression or anxiety. Doctors must rule out all the other possibilities before diagnosing ADD/ADHD.

Parents and teachers may be overeager for a diagnosis of ADD/ADHD, especially if children or teens have behavior problems that the adults are anxious to get under control. Everyone wants to come up with an answer, and they may be too quick to hit upon ADD/ADHD. They may even try to fit the teen's symptoms into the ADD/ADHD pattern when they don't really fit.

It won't help you with your problems to be treated for ADD/ADHD if you don't have it. If you are being tested, try to talk frankly to your doctor and parents and the evaluation team throughout the diagnostic process.

ADD/ADHD must be carefully diagnosed because many other problems, such as depression or learning disabilities, have similar symptoms. Thorough testing and evaluation may reveal a learning disability, a serious emotional disturbance, a hearing problem, or a speech or language difficulty. It is possible to have any of these difficulties and *also* to have ADD/ADHD. So how do you know if you have ADD/ADHD?

As a result ADD/ADHD may even be underdiagnosed for many teens. Their problems may be missed altogether, or be mistakenly attributed to other causes.

Symptoms

To diagnose ADD/ADHD, a health care professional requires information about you and your symptoms from a variety of sources. To identify symptoms, they refer to the American Psychiatric Association's *Diagnostic and Statistical Manual of Mental Disorders*, IV edition, the authority in defining mental health and developmental health difficulties.

As you can see from the lists below, which are summarized from the manual, ADD and ADHD symptoms are related but not exactly the same. For ADD or ADHD to be diagnosed, some problems with attention or impulsiveness must have started before the age of seven, even if they were not diagnosed then. The symptoms must have existed for more than six months, and they must affect you in at least two settings, such as home and school. They must interfere with how you should be functioning at your age, for example with your schoolwork. And they must not be the direct result of another problem, such as an anxiety disorder, although you may have other such problems.

ADD Symptoms

- Difficulty paying attention
- Difficulty sustaining attention
- Difficulty listening

- Difficulty completing tasks
- Difficulty with organizational skills
- Avoiding tasks requiring sustained effort
- Losing things
- Easily distracted
- Forgetting things.

ADHD Symptoms

- Fidgeting and squirming
- Leaving seat often
- Running or climbing excessively (in teenagers or adults, extreme restlessness)
- Difficulty with quiet leisure activities
- Being always on the go
- Talking excessively
- Blurting out answers
- Difficulty waiting turns
- Interrupting or intruding on others.

Evaluation

Not everyone fits neatly into one category or the other —ADD or ADHD. You may have symptoms from both at times.

If you have six or more of these symptoms for more than six months, a thorough assessment should be made to determine if you have ADD or ADHD. The following format is a common one for a health care professional to use for an evaluation:

- Parent interview
- Teacher interview
- Observation in classroom

- Student (child or teen) interview
- Behavior Rating Scales (completed by teacher and parents)
- Testing (intellectual, achievement, and fine-motor skills)
- Medical evaluation

Many experts have published Rating Scales. Ask your librarian to show you where they are kept.

Parents have a wealth of information about their children. They can tell the interviewer about the child's or teen's current symptoms and behavior. The interviewer will also want to know about the early development of the child, such as walking and talking. The parents will be asked if the young child listened, was impulsive, or was more active than other children. This kind of information is important in diagnosing ADD/ADHD.

Teachers are also a valuable source of information. They know how a student's attention span and activity levels compare to those of others students of his age. In addition, someone other than the teacher should observe the student in the classroom for more insight.

The interviewer will also speak to the teen or child to hear his description of the problems he is encountering and anything else he would like to discuss.

Parents and teachers fill out written questionnaires. These Behavior Rating Scales are lists of questions about how the child responds to certain activities and tasks. For example, a common question on the parents' list is, "Do you consider your child to be more active than most children his age?"

The student is often asked to take several tests. Some tests can help screen out or identify learning disabilities and other problems, both psychological and physical.

Intelligence tests help an evaluator to assess the student's level of ability. People with ADD/ADHD can have intelligence of any level—high, average, or low. For many years, people thought a person's intelligence was set in stone. We have now learned that ability level or intellectual level can be changed. Experiences and environment play a role in ability or intellectual level.

Achievement tests show the grade level at which the student is working. For example, a student can be working at a ninth-grade level in math and a second-grade level in reading.

Fine-motor tests may consist of paper-and-pencil activities and other tests of the student's finger coordination and speed. Students with fine-motor difficulties are slow in completing their written work in the classroom. Handwriting is often poor in students with ADD/ADHD.

Finally, the teen or child should have a **medical exam** by a doctor who is experienced with ADD/ADHD.

All of the information gathered through this process makes possible a complete view of the teen or child. It is rather like looking at different parts of the person under a microscope and then putting all the pieces together to see the whole picture and make the diagnosis.

It can be a great relief to both the teen and the parents to find out that the teen *does* have ADD/ADHD. At last they all know that the problems are no one's fault. ADD/ADHD is a neurobiological disorder. Now that they know what the problem is, they can start to improve the situation.

FREDDY

Freddy had never been able to sit in one place for more than a few minutes. His teachers nicknamed him Flighty Freddy back in first grade. His parents called him Fidgety Freddy.

Everyone knew Freddy could do the work if he would just pay attention. Freddy's dad said he had been the same way in school. Freddy could still hear his dad's words as he talked to the new teachers every year. "You just have to hold him down. He can learn if you can get him to sit still long enough to pay attention." Then his dad would laugh.

In the summertime, Freddy's problems didn't seem so bad. There weren't as many rules to follow. But Freddy's problems at school got worse every year. He couldn't pay attention. He talked out of turn. As he got older, his homework assignments were longer and more complicated, and he couldn't finish them. He often got into trouble, and he wasn't happy.

Finally the school recommended that Freddy be tested for ADHD. The school psychologist talked to Freddy and his parents. She said they needed to gather a lot of information about Freddy. She would need to interview Freddy, his teachers, and his parents. His teachers and parents would fill out questionnaires to rate his behavior, and he would take several tests.

Freddy had a hard time sitting still for the tests. The psychologist let him take breaks, which helped. He didn't much enjoy the reading and answering the questions about what he had read, but it wasn't too bad.

Based on Freddy's tests, the interviews, and the rating scales, Freddy's doctor wrote an official diagnosis of Attention Deficit Hyperactive Disorder, or ADHD.

The doctor said that he would like to order some medication that should help improve Freddy's symptoms. He would start off prescribing small doses and carefully monitor Freddy's reactions. At the same time, the doctor said, Freddy would need to learn some special techniques to help him cope with his disorder and do better in school. He would need the help of his parents and teachers to use these techniques.

The school set a date for a conference with Freddy, his parents, and his teachers. They all talked to his counselor about developing a plan that would help Freddy manage his disorder and still learn with the rest of his class.

The funny thing was that while Freddy was being evaluated, his dad started thinking that maybe *he* had always had ADHD without knowing it. He had himself evaluated, and it turned out he was right. Now he and Freddy used some of the same kinds of behavior management techniques to help them deal with their symptoms.

CHAPTER 3

Medication to Help

Manage ADD/ADHD

I f you have been diagnosed with ADD/ADHD, your doctor will probably suggest that you try one or more of the medications commonly used to treat attention deficit disorders. Medication will not cure ADD/ADHD, and it will not control your behavior. What medication can do is help improve your symptoms. An improvement in your symptoms, such as lengthening your attention span, will make it easier for you to work on the ADD/ADHD-related problems you encounter at school, at home, and with your friends.

Medication, if used, will be only one part of the treatment of your ADD/ADHD. Complete treatment of attention deficit disorders must be *multimodal*. This means that they must be treated by several methods at the same time. A multimodal treatment plan might include medication, therapy or counseling for you and your family, behavior management, and a school plan. Other parts of the multimodal plan are discussed further in Chapter 4.

Medication can be very helpful for about three quarters of children with ADD/ADHD. Others may experience side effects or find that it doesn't improve their symptoms. Your doctor may want you to try several different medications to find the best one for you.

The dosage needed varies from person to person. Your doctor will prescribe a certain dosage to start. Then you, your parents, and teachers will observe your behavior for several days. The dosage will be adjusted until you reach the best level.

You and your parents should learn about ADD/ADHD medications before deciding whether you should try them. If you do decide to try medication, it is important to pay attention to how it is affecting you. Each person's body reacts differently to various drugs. The Appendix has a fact sheet published by CH.A.D.D. (Children and Adults with Attention Deficit Disorder) about medications and their effects. In addition, the accompanying monitoring chart can help you keep track of the doses of each drug you take and monitor any side effects. You should also ask your doctor to discuss with you and your parents how often you should take your medication. You may find it best to maintain the same level of medication in all situations year-round. Some teens do better varying their medication, depending on whether they're at home, at school, or on vacation. You should not make any changes in your prescribed course of medication without talking to your doctor.

Medication Monitoring Charts

The person being treated, the parents, and teachers should all fill out charts like these because reactions and behavior may vary throughout the day. Give the completed charts to the doctor who prescribed the medication at your next visit. He or she will use the information to adjust the dosage and type of medication.

MEDICATIONS DOSAGE
(List all medications below)

Name: _____   Date: _____

Birthdate: _____   Age: ___   Grade: _____

Medication	Dose	Frequency	Time Taken

Variations in frequency or other comments:

_____

_____

REACTIONS AND BEHAVIOR
(Note all reactions and behavior below)

Day:
Date:
Time:
Place Observed:
Name of person filling out chart:

Behaviors	Better	Worse	No Change	Comments
Social				
Peer Interaction				
Parent Interaction				
Teacher Interaction				
Task-Related				
Listening				
Inattention				
Impatience				
Distractibility				
Completing Work				
Handling Interruptions				
Physical/Emotional				
Fidgety				
Impulsiveness				
Activity Level				
Moody				
Bored				
Difficulty with Rules/Authority				

SIDE EFFECTS
(Note all side effects experienced)

Day:
Date:
Time:
Place experiences observed:
Name of person filling out chart:

Social	Behaviors	Better	Worse	No Change	Comments
Nervousness					
Sleeplessness					
Vomiting					
Skin rash					
Dizziness					
Headaches					
Depression					
Loss of Appetite					
Irritability					
Confusion					
Stomachaches					
Excessive Crying					
Motor/Vocal Tic					
Other (describe)					

The drugs used to treat ADD/ADHD are not addictive. But they can have side effects for some people, and in a small percentage of people serious effects such as Tourette's syndrome, a neurological disorder involving involuntary movements and behavior. That is why it is important to pay attention to how any medication affects you.

Overmedication

There are other reasons to be cautious about using medication. As we saw in Chapter 2, ADD/ADHD may be incorrectly diagnosed in many young people. This means that they may take medication for a condition they don't have. This is *not* a good idea. In other cases, some young people who do have a disorder could have first tried to treat it without medication. Their doctors may have been too quick to prescribe medication, especially if their parents and teachers were desperate to see an improvement in behavior. Finally, it is important that the doctor determine the minimum dosage needed. Taking more medication than you need can affect you negatively.

You may hate the idea of using any drugs, or you may be embarrassed about taking them, especially at school. Your parents may have negative feelings about letting you take medication and be concerned about the effect on your overall health. Your concerns and worries are very important. You and your parents should carefully discuss the pros and cons of the ADD/ADHD medications with your doctor and the other people who have been involved in the diagnosis.

Write a list of questions that you and your parents want to ask your doctor. Take it to your appointment so you won't forget to ask anything. Write down the answers too. Don't be afraid to ask the doctor to explain anything you don't understand. ADD/ADHD is a complicated topic, and the answers are very important—more important to you than to anyone else. Here are some questions to start your list.

1. What are the possible short-term negative effects of the medication?
2. What are the possible long-term negative effects?
3. How will we find the lowest possible dosage I can take?
4. How would this drug interact with other substances I might take, such as cold medicines and caffeine?
5. Should I take the medication all the time, or just on school days?

6. Do I need to get the medication in the middle of the day at school from the school nurse?
7. What happens if I forget to take my medication? Should I take my next dose at the regular time?
8. How often will we evaluate my continuing to use the drugs?
9. When can I or my parents call you if we have new questions about the medication?
10. How can I find out about the costs of the drugs and whether our medical insurance plan will cover them?

If you or your parents feel that your doctor is urging the use of medication too quickly, when nonmedical methods could be tried first, or if you or your parents have any lingering doubts after speaking with your doctor, you can always seek a second medical opinion.

You can get more information about ADD/ADHD medications from the support groups listed in the Help List and from some of the books listed. The more you educate yourself about ADD/ADHD, the more carefully you can decide whether or not to try medication.

Stimulants

Stimulant medications are most often prescribed for ADD/ADHD. For people without ADD/ADHD, a stimulant drug increases activity. For those with attention deficit disorders, however, stimulants have a very different effect. Their general positive effect can include:

- increased attention
- increased short-term memory
- increased control of impulses

- increased visual-motor coordination
- less oppositional behavior
- decreased aggressiveness
- decreased talkativeness
- more task-oriented behavior.

General possible side effects (short-term or long-term) of stimulants can include:

- reduced appetite
- sleep problems
- weight and growth pattern suppression
- nausea, headaches, dizziness, abdominal discomfort
- motor or vocal tics, such as Tourette's Syndrome, especially if there is a family history of tics.

Stimulant Medications for ADD/ADHD

Ritalin (generic name: methylphenidate)
Ritalin is the most commonly prescribed drug for ADD/ADHD. Its effects can be seen within 30 to 90 minutes after being taken orally. Ritalin is available in tablet form in doses of 5 milligrams (mg), 10 mg, 20 mg, and sustained release SR 20 mg.

Dexedrine (generic name: dextroamphetamine)
Some people with ADD/ADHD do better with Dexedrine than with Ritalin. This drug is available in 5-mg tablets, as well as in time-released capsules. The user generally can notice the effects within 30 to 90 minutes.

Cylert (generic name: pemoline)
Cylert is slower-acting but longer-lasting than Ritalin or Dexedrine. Cylert may take three to six weeks to reach

maximum effectiveness. Liver function tests are recommended prior to and periodically during use.

Nonstimulant Medications for ADD/ADHD

Catapres (generic name: clonidine)

Catapres is an antihypertensive drug that has recently been used for some hyperactive persons, but not for those who have ADD without hyperactivity. It is available in tablets or as a patch worn on the skin like a Band-Aid. The effects are seen within 30 to 60 minutes. Nausea, rashes, drowsiness, dryness of the nose and mouth, Tourette's Syndrome, constipation, and lightheadedness are some of the possible effects.

Tofranil (generic name: imipramine) and Norpramin (generic name: desipramine)

Sometimes people with ADD/ADHD are depressed or feel too many side effects from the stimulants they are taking. They may be given antidepressants, such as Tofranil or Norpramin. These drugs can also be helpful in reducing hyperactivity and aggression. Side effects can include sensitivity to sunlight, tiredness, mild stomach disturbances, and sleep disorders. These drugs can affect the user's heart rate, so the doctor must monitor the heart carefully.

DELBERT

Delbert sat in the office listening to the doctor tell his mother that he should try Ritalin to help with his ADHD. He felt like a case in a textbook, as if he were not even there. He decided that he wanted a say in his treatment and went about it in his usual way. "No!" he yelled. "I don't want to take drugs!"

The doctor said, "You seem pretty angry today, Delbert."

Delbert's mother said, "Delbert is angry about a lot of things. Will this medicine help him control his anger?"

"It should," the doctor replied. "Delbert, you have a history of anger and restlessness, and you've been suspended from school several times for starting fights or for uncontrollable behavior. I know you have started counseling and behavior management, which is great. But I think it is time to try something else too. I know your complete medical history, and I think you are a good candidate for medication. I recommend trying the Ritalin and continuing the counseling and behavior management. These should help you feel less aggressive and able to focus and concentrate on things like homework, reading, and listening when a person is speaking to you."

The doctor explained that he would carefully monitor the program, and that the prescription could not be refilled without his approval. He assured both Delbert and his mother that Delbert would not become addicted to the medication. He suggested that Delbert should try Ritalin first and then Dexedrine, to see which was more helpful.

"Let's try it for a week and see how it goes. In the middle of the week we'll adjust the dosage if necessary. We'll make an appointment for next week and decide then whether you should stay on the medication or not. How does that sound?"

Delbert thought about it and decided to try it for a week. He nodded in reluctant agreement. He wasn't wild about the idea of having to take drugs. He didn't want to take them in front of his classmates or friends. But then again, if they could improve his ADHD symptoms, maybe he'd have more friends.

After just a week, Delbert found that the Ritalin made a noticeable difference in his ability to cope with his disorder. He decided to continue using it. The medication made it possible for him to concentrate on improving his behavior and his schoolwork. Slowly he started making friends again. People could see that he had changed and that he was really trying to get along. His self-esteem improved with every new success. He continued working closely with his counselor, his mother, his teachers, and his doctor. By the end of three years, he had a part-time job, had improved his grades, and had a serious girlfriend. He knew that he had achieved all these successes himself, but he felt that the Ritalin had been a big help.

Alternatives to Medication

Although medication can be of great help to many teens with ADD/ADHD, not everyone benefits from medication and not everyone wants to use it. Researchers continue to look for ways to improve ADD/ADHD symptoms without medication. For example, some people are using EEG biofeedback (electroencephalogram). This is a method of measuring certain activity in parts of the brain and then training the person to alter his brain wave activity to improve attention span and decrease hyperactivity.

Other people have studied the treatment of ADD/ADHD through the control of diet. Some treatments eliminate substances such as sugar and food additives. Others focus on increasing the intake of certain vitamins and minerals. To date, these studies have not provided evidence of effectiveness that is accepted by most mainstream experts. Some alternative treatments are considered very controversial; others are considered to be worth more research. Some appear to be useful for small numbers of people with ADD/ADHD.

For teens with ADD/ADHD and their parents, it can be very tempting to try the latest experimental treatment, especially when someone else says that it helped them. It is wise to proceed cautiously, to read all the available information pro and con, and to discuss all possible treatments with trusted health care professionals.

Whether or not you use medication in the treatment of your ADD/ADHD, you will certainly need to use several other methods of management, as we shall see in the following chapter.

CHAPTER ◇ 4

Techniques to Help
Manage ADD/ADHD

A multimodal treatment of ADD/ADHD is extremely important to ensure your success. This means using several methods at the same time. You cannot rely only on medication. Multimodal treatments may include:

- behavior management techniques
- organizational techniques
- an educational plan for you to use in school and for homework
- counseling or therapy for you or your parents or both
- medication.

Multimodal treatment requires the cooperation of you, your parents, your teachers and school staff, your doctor, and your counselor or therapist. ADD/ADHD is not a problem that you have just at home or at school. It affects you in many areas and in many ways, and it must be treated as such for you to get the best possible results.

Behavior Management Techniques

Once you have been diagnosed with ADD/ADHD, your counselor, therapist, or other professional trained in ADD/ADHD can help you and your parents develop a behavior management plan. This might include.

- identifying the specific behavior you need to change
- setting up a structured system of immediate rewards and penalties for each time you show a particular appropriate or inappropriate behavior
- making a specific plan on how to avoid unconstructive arguments and fights and to manage your anger.

Organizational Techniques

Teens with ADD/ADHD are frequently disorganized. You may lose things, forget dates, and do incomplete homework. Your counselor can help you develop methods to keep track of important information and tasks by using simple tools such as special notebooks, color-coded files, and clock-timers. These can be a big help in compensating for some of your symptoms and improving your performance in school.

Educational Plan

Students with ADD/ADHD usually need some classroom changes in order to perform at their best. These changes can range from sitting up front in the classroom to special structures for taking tests or extra help from the teacher. Students who also have learning disabilities may need special education classes.

Two federal laws pertain to the educational needs of students with ADD/ADHD. One is the Individuals with Disabilities Education Act (IDEA); the other is Section 504 of the Rehabilitation Act of 1973. Because many schools do not realize that ADD/ADHD is a disability, the U.S. Department of Education issued a "Policy Clarification Memorandum" in 1991 to make it clear that ADD/ADHD qualifies students for reasonable accommodations if their disorder severely affects their performance in school.

Whether a student qualifies for this help is determined by a complete evaluation of the student's school experience. Your parents should write a letter requesting that the school do an evaluation to see if you can receive educational help under these laws.

If you do qualify, you and your parents and school will create a 504 Plan to meet your particular learning needs. Your educational plan can be one of your most useful tools to cope with ADD/ADHD in school. It is important that you get all the help to which you are legally entitled in order to develop your plan and put it into practice. Your educational rights are discussed in Chapter 5.

Counseling and Therapy

Therapy may be recommended by your doctor. Therapy can be useful to a teen with ADD/ADHD who is also experiencing depression, low self-esteem, or other psychological problems. Your parents may also benefit from therapy to discuss all the stresses and strains that coping with ADD/ADHD puts on them.

A counselor trained in ADD/ADHD is another person who can help. A counselor can help you create and follow treatment plans like the ones discussed above. You can learn about proven treatment plans and tailor them to your individual needs by working with a professional counselor.

Support Groups

You and your parents should also find out about local support groups for parents and children with ADD/ADHD. Call or write the national organizations listed in the Help List at the end of this book. They will send you information about membership fees and what local chapters may be near you. One national group is CH.A.D.D., or Children and Adults with Attention Deficit Disorder. CH.A.D.D. has over 20,000 members and 500 local chapters nationwide. It publishes very useful fact sheets about different aspects of ADD/ADHD.

Educating yourself about your disorder is one of the best ways you can learn to manage it. The support groups can help you stay up-to-date on the latest research. Most people also find it helpful to talk to others who have similar problems, and you may find that you enjoy meeting other people with ADD/ADHD.

JUDITH

Judith and her parents decided to try to treat her ADD without medication. Judith was highly motivated and thought she could work on her symptoms using organizational skills, behavior management, and counseling. She and her parents met with a private therapist to create a behavior management program, including organizational skills. After that, Judith met with the therapist by herself once a week.

Judith said that completing her homework was a major problem. She either forgot what the assignment was, forgot to take her books home, forgot to study, or forgot to take the homework to school the next day. She and the therapist devised a homework organization plan for Judith to use with her teachers' help. Judith chose rewards and punishments to motivate her to follow the plan. Her punishment was not talking on the phone with her friends if she did not meet her daily goals. Her reward was hanging out with her friends on Saturdays if she did meet her goals.

Judith bought a notebook just for homework assignments and took it to every class. She wrote down each assignment and asked her teacher to check it after class. At the end of the day, she looked in the notebook to get all of the needed books to take home.

As she finished each assignment at home, her mother put her initials next to the listing, and the completed assignment was placed on a special table by the front door. When Judith turned in each assignment, the teacher initialed the notebook.

Judith had six classes a day, each with homework. She had been turning in an average of one assignment a day at the beginning of the program. Her first goal was to complete and turn in two assignments a day. By the fifth week she was to turn in all six assignments on time each day.

Judith wasn't thrilled about having to get all of those initials. After several months, she was able to complete all the assignments without the reminders. Still, she continued to use the notebook to keep herself organized and help her remember what to study each day.

Judith worked hard and was successful. She was proud of herself. She continued with therapy sessions for the rest of the year, working on other ADD/ADHD problems at home and in her social life. By the second year, she called her therapist only if she felt overwhelmed. The organizational skills she learned helped her to deal with many aspects of her life.

JOEY

Joey was doing research at the library. He had to write a paper about ADD/ADHD. It wasn't his idea; one of his teachers had assigned him the topic. As he looked through the books and articles on ADD/ADHD, Joey felt he was reading about himself. He knew that he had a short attention span and that it had always been hard for him to sit still. He was always fidgeting in his seat and getting things in and out of his desk. It wasn't that he was trying to create problems. Sometimes he just wondered where he had put something and decided to look in his desk for it. School was boring anyway. Sometimes things his teachers mentioned reminded him of something else. When the teacher accused him of not listening, it seemed to Joey that he *had* been listening.

One book he read said that distractibility was a symptom of ADD/ADHD. Yes, Joey felt that he had a distractibility problem too. If the student next to him began tapping his pencil, Joey couldn't hear the teacher. All he could hear was the pencil tapping. Sometimes he heard the teacher talking in the class-room next door instead of his own teacher. The school had checked his hearing several times. Maybe it wasn't his hearing. Maybe it was distractibility.

The subject of medication caught Joey's attention. "It would be great if I could take a pill and change everything," he thought. As Joey read on, he found that medication was helpful for many teens with ADD/ADHD, but not all. He decided to ask his doctor about it.

Next Joey read about losing track of time. He knew he often tried to do too many things in one day instead of focusing on the important ones. He copied the Time-Monitoring Chart to help him see how he used his time every day.

Joey kept reading. He found some behavior management techniques for ADD/ADHD called "cognitive control strategies." He thought maybe he could try them himself and see if they worked. He started to take notes:

1. Monitor myself during class or when reading by making tally marks on a piece of paper whenever I drift from material.
2. Take notes in class or from the book. Have the teacher check to see if I wrote down the most important things.
3. To remember things better: Make mental pictures. Repeat things over and over. Make associations by thinking of things the subject reminds me of. Make acronyms out of the first letters of words to make remembering easier.
4. Make note cards and highlight important information.

5. Make maps or diagrams to see how ideas are connected.
6. Develop a study schedule. Make a chart to keep track of time to study each subject.
7. Ask a counselor or teacher to help me with a study guide and decide on learning strategies to study things.

The books and articles Joey read suggested that the way you dealt with ADD/ADHD could help you be successful. That was interesting. Joey thought that no one is perfect in life. Everyone has some problem to compensate for. Maybe his problems were related to ADD/ADHD. He decided to show his parents the research he had done and ask for an appointment with their family doctor.

TIME-MONITORING CHART

On a typical busy day, keep a Time-Monitoring Chart. Write down all the things you do.

Activity	Time	Purpose of Activity	Results	Emotional Feeling About Activity
____	____	____	____	____
____	____	____	____	____
____	____	____	____	____
____	____	____	____	____
____	____	____	____	____
____	____	____	____	____

——————— ———— ————————— ———— —————————

——————— ———— ————————— ———— —————————

1. What did you accomplish? ————————————————

2. How many activities did you enjoy? ——————————

3. Were you happy or unhappy? ——————————————
   (State what made the difference)

4. Now plan how to change the ways you use your time.
   ————————————————————————————————————

(Your parents or counselor can help you.)

CHAPTER ◇ 5

School Can Be a Real Drag: How to Make It Better

Most ADD/ADHD teenagers have felt rejected and disappointed in school. School is a real drag for them a lot of the time.

Schools are often rigid, structured places where students have to sit quietly in one place for long periods. An ADHD teen finds it difficult to sit quietly and consequently is often in conflict with the adults who are trying to enforce the rules. ADD/ADHD students also have trouble concentrating and paying attention. They tend to miss a lot in class, including homework assignments. Some students even convince themselves that the teacher never gave the assignment. Often, they really didn't hear what the teacher said. That's the nature of ADD/ADHD.

Legal Rights and Realities

Schools are required by law to accommodate the needs of students with ADD/ADHD who meet certain criteria. Under the Individuals with Disabilities Education Act, students with ADD/ADHD may qualify for reasonable accommodations to meet the student's personalized needs. Under the other law, Section 504 of the Rehabilitation Act of 1973, ADD/ADHD students may qualify to have accommodations made for them within their regular classrooms.

This is the way the system works when everything goes right: Your teachers or your parents think that your problem may be caused by ADD/ADHD and that it is having major effects on your schooling. Your parents make a written request to the school to have you evaluated and diagnosed. The school has a team of people carry out the required tests, at no cost to your family. Most schools require a medical diagnosis. If you are diagnosed with ADD/ADHD and if the evaluation shows that it significantly affects your school performance, you, your parents, and the people designated by the school write a special plan for your needs in school. For instance, if you need reasonable accommodations, these will be specified. Or if you need changes in your regular classroom, such as extra time to take tests, this will be written in your plan. Then you and your teachers and everyone involved will follow the plan to improve your ability to learn and to do your work. At the same time, you will use other treatment methods for your ADD/ADHD, such as behavior management techniques.

In many schools students get help quickly and find the staff wonderfully supportive and eager to improve the situation. But in other schools reality may be quite different. If your school is understaffed, underfunded, and overcrowded, it may be slow and inefficient giving you the help you're entitled to. The teachers may be responsible for so many students that they just don't have enough time to give everyone individual attention. Or the people in your school may not understand ADD/ADHD or their legal obligation to help you. And in any school there may be people who just don't care enough to do what they are supposed to do.

Some parents decide to have the evaluation and diagnosis done by professionals who are not connected with the school. Then they must pay the fees themselves. If you and your parents choose this route, you still will need for your school to accept the evaluation and diagnosis and to make the changes you need.

Getting your school's cooperation may take persistence, letters, and phone calls. It may require educating the school staff if they are open to receiving information about ADD/ADHD. It could even require taking legal action against the school. If your school is not cooperating, contact one of the ADD/ADHD support groups listed in the back of this book. Through them you can find out more about obtaining your legal rights and how other parents and students got their schools to work with them.

If they are not familiar with current information on ADD/ADHD, teachers and administrators should be given a fact sheet explaining these disorders. CH.A.D.D. (Children and Adults with Attention Deficit Disorder), a national support group, has published an excellent article that is short, to the point, and updated regularly. It is reprinted in the appendix. You can also call or write CH.A.D.D. and ask about its fact sheets for teachers and about your educational rights. You may also want to show your teachers a copy of this book.

CASEY

Casey's father was in the military service. Her family moved from place to place as her father was restationed in different parts of the United States and in other countries. It is hard on kids to start at new schools all the time. It was especially hard for Casey because she had ADD and a learning disability. Every time she changed schools, she had to explain herself all over again to new people, and she had to learn a new routine.

Casey had learned from experience to take the initiative herself when she enrolled in a new school. She went directly to the assistant principal or school counselor and gave them a packet that contained the following items:

1. Letter from a medical doctor with her diagnosis of ADD and her medication requirements. Casey needed to take medication at school in the middle of the day.
2. Test results, which included the best learning approach for Casey.
3. Individualized Education Plan (IEP) from her previous school.
4. Letter from a past teacher explaining what worked best in the classroom.
5. Article from Children and Adults with Attention Deficit Disorder (CH.A.D.D.), giving a brief description of ADD/ADHD.

Casey found that the people in some schools were ready to work with her. In other schools, they did not understand or were not helpful, and she had to try harder to get their cooperation. Before she entered the classroom, she requested a conference with the principal or assistant principal, the counselor, teachers, her parents, and herself. Casey preferred to take the initiative and do this herself. Casey had a friend named Tawanda who had ADD/ADHD and who had also changed schools a lot. Tawanda always had her parents make the request because she thought the authorities paid more attention to her parents, and it made things easier. Each girl found the best approach for her own situation.

Casey explained her specific problems in the conference and talked about her best learning style, which was a visual approach to learning. She explained that she had poor listening skills and found it hard to remember facts. She did better if she could see the material on overhead projectors, visual aids, or the blackboard. This information was also in her IEP.

In addition to explaining the support she needed from them, Casey asked what their expectations were for her. She tried to be reasonable. She realized that teachers have a lot of students to think about. She tried to be assertive about her needs, but never aggressive or rude.

After talking to everyone she would work with, Casey started school. She used some of the organizing and listening techniques her original counselor had worked out with her. At her current school, she was pleased to find she would be in the same classes as Carlos, a student her age who had ADD/ADHD. Casey and Carlos soon became good friends. Sharing experiences with each other made them feel less alone.

CARLOS

Mr. Jordan was trying to ignore Carlos. He could hear the boy tapping his pencil, shuffling papers in his desk, and whispering to the girl next to him. It seemed to Mr. Jordan that Carlos was purposely trying to irritate him. When Carlos's book crashed loudly to the floor, Mr. Jordan exploded. "Carlos, take your things and go to the office to work. You obviously can't work in here."

The room grew quiet. Carlos felt himself growing numb. When he got into trouble he always went numb so he didn't feel so hurt. As Carlos picked up his things, his pencil and notebook fell to the floor. He nervously picked them up. Everyone was watching. Mr. Jordan just stood and waited, looking angry. Carlos was afraid to ask what the assignment was going to be. He knew he wouldn't be able to do it anyway without hearing Mr. Jordan explain it in class. And then he would be in trouble again when he showed up without the assignment. Carlos was devastated.

It seemed to Carlos as if nothing worked out at school, no matter how hard he tried to manage his ADHD. As he trudged down the hall to the office, he met Ms. Washington, the school counselor. She said, "Carlos, you certainly look down today."

Before he knew it, he had told her the whole story. She went to the office with him and helped him get started on another assignment. Before she left, she assured him that she would help him get things worked out. Later that day she found Carlos and took him to Mr. Jordan's room. Carlos had trouble looking Mr. Jordan in the eye. Ms. Washington said she and

Mr. Jordan had been talking. She asked Carlos to explain what he had been trying to do to cope with his ADHD. She helped him and Mr. Jordan draw up some guidelines that could work for both of them. The guidelines they agreed upon were these:

1. Carlos would try to be the first one in the room and to get his materials organized before class began.
2. Carlos would write down the assignments.
3. Carlos would take notes during the class period. (Writing was difficult for Carlos, so he knew his notes would be brief. If note-taking became a distraction for him, he would tell Mr. Jordan, and it could be discontinued.)
4. Carlos would raise his hand or hold his pencil up when he needed help or to ask a question.
5. Mr. Jordan would walk by and pause beside Carlos's desk twice during each class period to remind him to concentrate. He wouldn't say anything to draw attention to Carlos.
6. Mr. Jordan would remember to compliment Carlos privately when he did appropriate things.
7. From time to time Carlos and Mr. Jordan would discuss whether the guidelines were working or if they should adjust them.

Carlos saw Ms. Washington in the hall a few days later. She took one look at him and said, "Hey, I like that big smile on your face these days." Carlos laughed and said, "Yeah, Mr. Jordan's really cool."

*　　　*　　　*

Sometimes it can be difficult to approach a particular teacher. Like Carlos, you may need to ask another adult to speak to the teacher first or to be there when you talk to him or her. If you feel that the teacher is correcting you all the time, you may get so angry that you start to blame the teacher for everything. It helps if you level with the teacher or administrator and explain how terrible it makes you feel to be singled out for criticism in the classroom. Ask them to talk to you in private, and say that you will do your best to change. Together the two of you can come up with some guidelines, like Carlos's list, to help you focus in class. Remember, if the first plan does not work, ask your teacher or counselor to help you change it. Don't be discouraged. Draw up some guidelines or signals to try until you get to the right choice for *you*.

Homework

Guidelines like the ones Carlos used can help if you don't know the assignment or get mixed up about it. But even when you are clear on the assignment, you still may not know where to start. It is easier to tackle your homework if you organize it first.

It is important to take the following three Giant Steps of Change: "OL & P"

Step One: Organize Yourself
Step Two: Listen
Step Three: Proofread

Step 1. First of all, you have to find a way to organize yourself. Buy the most fantastic, fun notebook you have ever seen. Copy the following form into the front of the notebook. Use one form for each day of the school week. It is important to put your name on the top line. Write it with a sense of pride and ownership. This is *yours*.

_____'s Homework Assignment					
Week of: _____ Day: _____ Date: _____					
	English	*Math*	*Science*	*Social Studies*	*Other Subject*
I listened to the teacher in class (Yes/ Some/No)					
Assignment					
Time estimated to do homework					
Homework completed?					
Proofread for errors?					
I took the time for my writing to be neat (Yes/ Some/No)					

Step 2. The second step is to listen carefully in class and write the assignment down. Once you let your mind wander off the subject in class, it is hard to start listening again. Ask your teacher to give you signals, such as touching you on the shoulder or pausing by your desk, to recall your attention at intervals. Try to train yourself to keep listening even if you find what the teacher is saying dull and boring. One way to improve your concentration skills is to write down the main words the teacher says. This is called taking notes. If you're taking notes, you have to concentrate. It's hard to write fast enough to catch everything, so don't worry about getting every word. Just get the most important ones. As your listening skills improve, you will miss less information and fewer assignments. Ask your teacher to see if you wrote the assignment down correctly, just to be sure.

Back to Step 1, organization. If it is a long assignment, break it down into sections that you can handle one by one. Write each section on your daily Homework Assignment Report. Next write how long you think it will take you to do each section, as well as the time you need for the entire assignment.

Now play "Beat the Clock." Get all your homework supplies together in the best area you have to concentrate, away from distractions. You will need a timing device, such as a kitchen timer. Set the timer for the length of time you have estimated for the first section. See if you can finish before the timer rings.

As you finish each section, put a check mark in the completed category on your form. This will give you a sense of accomplishment. Continue with each section until you finish the entire assignment.

Step 3. Finally, after you have completed the entire assignment, go back and proofread and double-check for errors. After you have corrected your mistakes, mark off the "proofread" line in your report form.

You will be surprised how rapidly you have completed the entire homework for the day. Strange as it may seem, breaking it into parts and using a timer will actually save you time.

With all of the negative experiences and only a few positive experiences associated with school, ADD/ADHD students often feel that school is a real drag. Can this be turned around? *Yes!* But only by you, the student. You must take control of your life. Ask for all the help you need, and then take charge of your own school experience.

CHAPTER 6

Dealing with Your Family

D oes your home sometimes feel like a battleground? The teen years can be troublesome in any family. For teens with ADD/ADHD, maintaining good relationships with parents and brothers and sisters may sometimes seem impossible.

To make it more difficult, you may have a parent or sibling who also has ADD/ADHD. As many as 70 percent of people with ADD/ADHD have someone else in their family with an attention deficit disorder. Like their children, parents with ADD/ADHD may be impulsive, impatient, and easily frustrated. This makes the situation at home harder for everyone.

Get Outside Help

If you and your family feel locked in a struggle, the best way to break out of it may be to go outside the family for help and a better perspective.

Whether they have ADD/ADHD themselves or not, encourage your parents to join a support group. Tell them that you know how hard it is for them to cope with your disorder, and that talking to other parents of ADD/ADHD children may give them ideas and help them feel more optimistic that you can improve the situation. They may also find counseling or therapy helpful.

A support group and counseling or therapy can be a big help to you too. Just finding out that you are not alone in your special problems is a big relief. You can also get some ideas on how to improve life at home.

If you have already been diagnosed with ADD/ADHD, you probably know that your parents will play an important role in helping you learn to manage the disorder. But perhaps you have a parent with a problem such as alcoholism or drug abuse. Or maybe your parents work so hard to pay the bills that they are just too exhausted to give you the help you need. If your parents are unavailable to you for any reason, it is all the more important that you find other adults to rely on for guidance and support with your ADD/ADHD. Make a list of adults you could consult for different kinds of help and support. Do you have a sympathetic relative, a school counselor, a teacher, a doctor, or a clergyperson you could talk to? You may even decide to ask them to talk to your parents for you.

To find an ADD/ADHD support group near you, call or write to one of the organizations listed in the Help List and ask them for information. For help with alcoholism in the family, call the national number of Alcoholics Anonymous. There are groups to help with many kinds of family problems. You can also ask your school counselor or doctor where you can get help for your family.

SUSAN

Susan and her mother were very close, but they did have their moments. Sometimes they had major clashes. Susan's mother was a single parent who had been diagnosed with ADHD when she was in high school. Susan was diagnosed with ADHD when she was very young. Her pediatrician said she did not need medication. Susan and her mother both coped with their disorder by using behavior management techniques. But now that Susan was a teenager, it seemed as though she and her mother were fighting all the time. She was also having more difficulty with school and her friends. Her teachers suggested that she needed more help with her ADHD.

Susan and her mother decided to consult another doctor, Dr. Sullivan. The doctor said that she would like Susan to try Ritalin. She said she would ask Susan's teachers and mother to observe Susan carefully while she was trying the medication. She would need to adjust the dosage several times and try different medications to find the best one. Dr. Sullivan also arranged for Susan and her mother to go to therapy. They went to sessions together twice a month to work out their mutual problems. Susan went by herself the other two weeks of the month.

The therapist helped them discuss many of their feelings and conflicts. She gave them practical advice about how to resolve their disagreements instead of letting them get out of control. For instance, they agreed on a "zone out" instead of a "clash out." Whenever either of them felt tension rising, she had the option of calling "zone out" the way a referee calls "time out" in a ball game. Then they each went to separate places. Later they discussed the situation when they were both calmer and better able to focus. They also learned how to avoid getting into some arguments by using the techniques outlined below.

Avoid Trip Phrases

You can start improving relations at home by seeing how the conflicts arise. For instance, how do your arguments start? Parents and children say certain things to each other that "trip their switches," making the other person angry. Before they know it, they are having another argument. Does this sound like you? Make up your own list and ask your parents to make one too. Then, using the suggestions below for ideas, you and your parents can agree on some alternatives to try. Some "trip phrases" and possible alternative solutions are listed:

Teenager: "You never listen to me or pay attention to what I say!"

Alternative: "I need to talk to you. Is this a good time?"
(If it is not a good time, agree on a specific time later when you can talk.)

Teenager: "I'm not a criminal. Why do you treat me this way?"

Alternative: Agree in advance for your parent to allow you to go to your room to calm down before discussing things when you are angry.

Teenager: "I get sick and tired of your always saying, 'Think before you act,' or 'Pay attention.'"

Alternative: Prearrange a hand signal or cue word.
                 When you see the hand signal or hear
                 the cue word, you know what it means
                 without your parent's nagging you.

Parent: "There you go, lying about your home-
                 work again."
Alternative: Put a table by the front door for com-
                 pleted homework. The teen puts it
                 there at a prearranged time for the
                 parent to check. If it is not placed
                 by the door in completed form by the
                 agreed-upon time, the parent tapes a
                 note on the teenager's door, "See you
                 tomorrow at 4:00 p.m." This means the
                 teenager is grounded the next evening
                 after school. No verbal comments are
                 needed. (It is critical that the teenager
                 know where to get help with the home-
                 work. Teenager and parent need to
                 discuss this with a school counselor
                 or teacher. Look into tutors or other
                 solutions if necessary.)

Parent: "Get up off your lazy duff and take the
                 trash out. Why do I have to remind you
                 of everything?"
Alternative: Put up a bulletin board listing chores
                 for everyone in the family, including
                 parents. Check off chores as they are
                 completed. Set time limits, so everyone
                 knows when things are to be done.

Respect Each Other

Parents want and expect the best for their children. A teenager may feel that he can never meet his parents' expectations. Or maybe he doesn't even want to be the kind of person his parents expect. He may become angry and resentful. Many clashes may be ahead. ADD/ADHD children have more trouble than most children saying and doing the things their parents want them to say and do.

Parents should continue to want and expect the best for their children, but they must also be in tune with the children. The parents' job is to discipline, structure, nurture, direct, love. They must help their children be the best they can be for their own individual personality and talents.

Teenagers need to realize that the parents' job also includes helping their children develop a sense of responsibility, loyalty, respect, and love for themselves and others. Parents must be consistent in enforcing reasonable limits and structure. Because it is hard for ADD/ADHD children to accept structure, parents and children must work with special cooperation to create and accept the necessary rules.

As a teenager you may look back on some mistakes your parents made with you and vow not to make the same mistakes with your children. Parents, too, realize mistakes that have been made in their lives. When they see their children starting to make the same mistakes, they may overreact and be too hard on their children. This makes the situation worse.

JUAN

Juan had a terrible argument with his mother. She said he could not go to a concert the following week because it was on a school night. The guidelines they had agreed on for coping with Juan's ADHD said he would stay home and do homework on weeknights. Juan was furious. He shouted, "I hate you. I wish you were not my mother. I never want to see you again in my whole life."

This hurt Juan's mother deeply. It also reminded her of how Juan's father used to sound before their divorce. She shouted back at Juan, "I wish you weren't my child. You are bad, just like your father. You will never amount to anything. Just leave me and see how far you can get on your own. Maybe then you'll learn to appreciate me."

Juan and his mother had taken a bad situation and made it worse. When they realized how angry they were getting, they could have taken time out to calm down. Juan could have asked his mother to make an exception about the concert. Or Juan's mother could have said something like, "I know you are very angry right now. You need to go to your room and calm down. Write down your feelings and thoughts more clearly. Then make a list of some suggestions if you think we need to change your ADHD guidelines. I will do the same thing. Later, when we have both calmed down, we'll look at what we have written and see if we can find a compromise."

It would also help for Juan's mother to get some counseling to help her understand her anger about the divorce. She would be less likely to take her anger out on Juan if she realized that she was really still mad at Juan's dad.

CHARLIE

Charlie was preoccupied in school. He was a special education student; he had a learning disability and he had ADHD. He needed to pay attention in class, but he couldn't concentrate. Charlie wished he was not in school, but he didn't know where else to go. He knew he could not go home. His dad was home drunk from the night before. Charlie had not been able to finish his homework because of his parents' fighting and his dad's drinking. He simply could not concentrate with all the yelling and doors banging. He didn't know how to stop it. He had tried to intervene in the past, but both parents ended up yelling at him. He had seen his dad hit his mother more than once. What if his mother got hurt worse than bruises? He knew he would feel he should have stopped his dad. But how could he? Charlie felt angry and ashamed. And he was worried about his little brother and sister.

"Charlie, are you with us today?" The loud voice of Mr. Bradshaw, the English teacher, cut into his thoughts. "Do you have your homework?"

Charlie said, "I was not able to finish it." Mr. Bradshaw said, "Charlie, please see Mr. Maxwell [the counselor] today."

After class, Charlie walked by Mr. Maxwell's office and hesitated at the door. Mr. Maxwell looked up and said, "Hello, Charlie. I've been wanting to talk to you. Can you come in for a few moments?"

Charlie told him Mr. Bradshaw had sent him. Mr. Maxwell said, "Several of your other teachers have also talked to me. You had been managing your ADHD so well since you started the medication and using the guidelines we worked out. But recently you've seemed to have a harder time concentrating. What is happening in your life?" Charlie remained silent. Mr. Maxwell continued. "Unless you tell me, I can't help you. My only alternative is to call your parents. Perhaps I should call your house now while you're here."

Charlie begged Mr. Maxwell not to call his house, muttering something about his dad being sick. He had never told anyone about his parents.

Mr. Maxwell continued, "I have wondered for some time whether your father might be having problems. If he is, the worst thing you can do is try to protect him. I understand the stress you are under, and I am here to help."

Charlie got very quiet. Then he started talking. As he talked, he felt a great relief. It was so good to be able to talk to someone who understood. After he finished telling his story, Mr. Maxwell said, "I will talk to your mother. She has to be part of this picture too. She will be mad at both of us at first. Later on, I think she'll be very proud of you for standing up and getting some help."

Mr. Maxwell was right. Charlie's mother was very angry and upset, but eventually she ended up getting counseling and going to Al-Anon. Charlie attended Alateen. These are groups that help people who have alcoholics in their families. His father continued drinking, but Charlie and his mother learned how to concentrate on taking care of themselves and the rest of the family.

Charlie completed the year without failing. It had been hard at first to discuss his father's problems with others, but Charlie was glad he had done it.

Now he could think about his own life again instead of always worrying about his family.

Like Charlie, you may have major problems with your family that you cannot work out alone. You need to take the big step of asking for help from other adults in your life.

Family Basics

All parents and children have conflicts. If you have ADD/ADHD, you may feel that your family conflicts never stop. But with everyone's cooperation, you can reduce the level of tension in your home. Write down these basic guidelines and tape them up where you will see them often at home:

- Identify and avoid your "trip phases."
- Separate and calm down before discussing an issue.
- Respect each other's roles and responsibilities in the family.
- Get outside help when needed.

Some organizations that can help are listed in the back of this book.

CHAPTER 7

Dealing with Your Friends

Do your friends understand you? Do you understand them? These are big questions. Throughout your life, you will depend on friends for many emotional and practical needs. And they will depend on you. Good friends are important to your happiness.

Most people have felt lonely and misunderstand at some point in their lives. Almost everyone grows apart from a friend or has disagreements. If you have ADD/ADHD, these things may happen more often. You may have to work more carefully at making friends and at keeping them.

In the past, potential friends may have avoided you because you seemed too aggressive. Or, depending on your particular ADD/ADHD symptoms, people may have felt you didn't listen to them or you were too spaced out. Learning to use behavior management techniques, as we discussed in Chapter 4, will help make you a better friend. For instance, knowing how to control your temper will prevent flare-ups and fights. A trained professional can help you with these important social skills. Medication may also be useful. Ask your doctor about this.

Who Are Your Friends?

While you work on improving your friendship skills, it would also be a good idea to figure out who your friends are now and whom you would like to have as friends. First, take stock of the friends you have. Copy the chart below. Write down the names of the people who best match each category. Also list their relationship to you (include your friends, mother, father, sister, etc.). Next rate how well you meet each other's needs (good, fair, poor).

	FRIENDSHIP CHART			
	Names	Relationship	How well do you they meet your needs?	How well do you meet their needs?
Who listens to you?				
Who gives you positive feedback by telling you what a fantastic person you are?				
Who provides challenges to help you do better in life?				

Who gives you
emotional support
when things do
not go well?

Who gives you
spiritual support?

Whom do you
play or hang
out with?

Whom do you
exercise with
(bike, ride, run,
play tennis or
basketball, etc.)?

After you have filled out the chart, look at the first
column to see if one or two names appear too frequently.
If so, this is like putting all your eggs in one basket. If the
basket gets dropped, you could have big problems. You
may want to consider making some new friends.

Now read the second column. Are you relying too
much on your family members? Or not enough?

Look at the third column to see if your friends are
meeting your needs. Check the next column to see how
well you rate yourself at meeting their needs. Is there
room for improvement in some cases?

If you don't think you have been doing your part, think
about how you could do better. If your friends are not
meeting your needs in some areas, could they do more?
Or should you think about making another friend? Remember, no one friend can meet all your needs. You
might expect your best friend to understand a lot about

you, to talk to you about everything, including your ADD/ADHD. A more casual friend might be someone you just play games with. Some people are friends only at school or work.

EDWARD

Edward was feeling depressed. It was raining. He was bored and couldn't think of anything fun to do. He had tried to get a job, but he was only 15. Every place he tried said he had to be 16 before they would talk to him. He couldn't call any of his friends because they were fed up with him. They liked his energy, but they said he was too moody and temperamental and never listened to what they wanted to do. Edward blamed his ADHD for his moods. He knew he needed to do more work on the social skills he had learned from his counselor, but he didn't feel like it.

Edward turned on the television to see what was on. Just then the telephone rang, but it was for his sister June. He irritably called her to the telephone. When June got off the phone, she said her friend was coming by to take her to the mall. She asked Edward if he wanted to go with them. Edward jumped at the chance to do something, even if it was with his sister.

At the mall, June and her friend went shopping. They told Edward to meet them in two hours. Edward strolled around the mall, looking into the store windows. It was always difficult for him to stay in one place. Not watching what he was doing, he bumped into another teenager. The other boy frowned. Edward felt himself getting angry, but instead he took a deep breath and apologized. He said, "You having a bad day too?" The other boy said,

"You better believe it. Nothing good has happened today." Edward said, "Me too."

They began talking. Edward tried hard to listen and not to interrupt. Suddenly he remembered the time. He and his new friend had been talking for an hour. He had to rush to meet June. He and Philip exchanged telephone numbers and made plans to get together.

Edward was in a good mood now. He had done something positive for himself. He had been the first to speak and to be friendly.

ADHD teenagers can be good friends to others. Sometimes they need to work at it. To develop new friends, you have to find ways to meet people. You may have to go out of your way to be friendly first, like Edward. Your school counselor will be able to tell you about groups of teenagers that meet regularly. Choose a group with interests similar to yours. There may be clubs for science, music, art, or religion, for example.

You should also know how to avoid making friends with the wrong people. It may be tempting to be friends with someone just because they like you or seem to accept you the way you are. But listen to people first. Are they trustworthy? If they lie about themselves or others, or if they talk about people behind their backs, they will probably do the same to you. Do they use drugs? You must think carefully before getting involved with people who drink or use drugs. Most people give in to peer pressure, the pressure that they feel to join in whatever everyone else around them is doing. Drinking or using drugs is not a good idea for anyone. It is especially dangerous if you are already on medication, such as Ritalin, as many people with ADHD are. Drugs react when they are mixed together in someone's system. The reaction is never positive, and sometimes it can be fatal. Consider your choice of friends carefully.

When you make friends with someone, you are finding out what they are like on the inside. The only way to find out is to establish a line of communication with them. You have to be able to talk openly with them. That takes trust. The more you get to know them, the more openly you may talk and the more trust you may feel. Friends will be glad to find out what you are really like on the inside. Your ADD/ADHD need not be an obstacle to friendship.

CHAPTER 8

Is This Forever?

Experts say that about two thirds of ADD/ADHD cases persist into adulthood. However, some symptoms may change or decrease. Because you will be in different situations as an adult, your ADD/ADHD may affect you in different ways. For example, you will no longer have to go to school (unless you want to), so you won't have all those rules to follow and all those authority figures telling you what to do. On the other hand, you will have a job and a boss to answer to, and you will need to manage your ADD/ADHD so that you can be successful at work.

Adults who have never had their ADD/ADHD diagnosed may continue to have problems at home, at work, and with friends. And they may be more prone to depression and to drug and alcohol abuse. They are unaware of the cause of their behavior—ADD/ADHD—so they don't know how to change.

But if you are already trying to understand and manage your ADD/ADHD, you may be able to cope even better as an adult, whether your symptoms seem to diminish or not as you grow older. You can be a happy, successful person.

You are investing in your future every time you improve your listening techniques, practice communicating with a friend, or even complete a homework assignment. You are creating a happier, more self-confident you by learning to manage your ADD/ADHD. The skills you are working on now—with school, friends, and family—are the skills you will need later for your job and your adult relationships. So your first preparation for a happy future is improving the present.

The next step is to dream about your future. Yes, people probably tell you that you dream too much. But we must do some dreaming about what we want so that we can plan how to achieve it. To dream is to have it once. To make your dream a reality is to have it twice. Copy the chart below. You can use it to start planning your future.

GOAL CHART

My current age _____
How old will I be in 10 years? _____

	My 10-year goals	Steps to take each year to reach my goals
Career goals		
Relationship goals		
Social goals		
Spiritual goals		

Career

Think of all the things you have ever imagined becoming. What dream career would you like to become a reality? Be sure to set your sights high enough. Many successful people have ADD/ADHD. It has been speculated that inventor and political leader Benjamin Franklin, British statesman Winston Churchill, scientist Albert Einstein, and perhaps even U.S. President Bill Clinton may have had attention deficit disorder (*Time*, July 18, 1994). Perhaps some of them even found ways to turn their disorder into an advantage by choosing careers in which their extra drive and energy were a big plus.

People with attention deficit disorders often do better in jobs that involve moving around physically. Some examples of jobs that can be more physically active are real estate or other sales jobs, restaurant work, jobs in the hotel/tourism industry, and some kinds of teaching and law. There are many other possibilities. Jobs that require a lot of paperwork and recordkeeping are usually more difficult choices.

Using your own goal chart, write down a ten-year career goal. Do you want to graduate from college? Do you want to graduate from a vocational-technical college? Do you want to work in a big corporation, or a small business, or a school, or in politics? Would you like to work with computers, or plants, or music, or people? If you were now what you dream of becoming, would you act differently? Would you walk or talk differently? If so, for the next week practice acting, walking, and talking as if you were whatever you chose for your ten-year career goal. See how it feels to be that special person you want to become. If you like the feeling, how can you make it happen?

ADD/ADHD can help you with extra energy, but you will have to devote extra work, commitment, and follow-through to make your dream become reality. Your school counselor can help you with career ideas. Fill in some ideas on your chart about what to accomplish each year to work toward your goal. What will you need to learn more about now? Science? Art? Health? Can you talk to adults you know about these jobs? What schools or colleges might you find out about?

Relationship and Social Goals

What do you dream of for your marriage or relationship goals in ten years? How will ADD/ADHD affect your relationships? The significant other person in your life will need to thoroughly understand your disorder. If you marry someone who thinks he or she can change you, chances are you will both be miserable. It would be a good idea for both you and your intended partner to talk to your family doctor or counselor before deciding to get married. Besides talking about your relationship with each other, you will need to discuss the fact that if you have children, there is a chance that they will have ADD/ADHD. How would you cope with this? Talking things through before marriage can improve your future happiness.

What can you do now to become a better partner in the future? You may not even know the person now with whom you will spend the rest of your life. But if you can imagine the kind of person you will look for, you can imagine the kind of person they will want you to be.

You can start practicing in all your relationships now to be that person. Can you be a better listener? Better able to communicate how you are feeling? Better at taking time out when you are angry? Better able to channel your energy and enthusiasm in positive directions?

These are some of the areas to work on now for good relationships and social goals. To be mentally healthy, we all need to be close to a group of friends or relatives. Whether you are thinking about friendships or romance, you can start to create a happier future—right now.

Spiritual Goals

The spiritual dimension of your life is also important. Developing your spiritual side can help you deal with despair, grief, or other strong feelings that most people encounter in their lives. A spiritual sense can give you a feeling of peace and fulfillment. It may seem strange to think of setting goals for spirituality. But if you lead a busy life, you may find you need to set aside some time specifically to let your spiritual thoughts and feelings develop. You may want to explore these through prayer, music, or worship in a religious group. You may prefer reflection or meditation, or spending time outdoors. Volunteering to help other people can also give you spiritual satisfaction. All of these can help you to feel part of something greater than just your own world.

FRANK

Dr. Simpson's words were still ringing in Frank's ears as he left the office. Frank's mother was quiet, too, as she walked beside him.

Finally his mother spoke, "How do you feel about Dr. Simpson's saying that your ADHD symptoms have improved so much?" Frank thought, then answered, "It was a surprise. He is right, though. Things have been a lot easier recently. It has been such a gradual change, I don't really know when it happened."

"I don't know when you changed either. But you are definitely different than when you were in elementary school and junior high school," his mother replied.

Frank was completing his first year of training at a vocational-technical school. He was making average or above-average grades. He was happy with himself and had made friends with some of his classmates. Frank had qualified for a scholarship, and the school had helped him get a part-time job. He was pleased to be putting himself through school because his parents didn't have the money to help him. One more year and Frank would be out on his own with a full-time job. He was looking forward to that time.

PETER

As Peter sat on the bank of the lake with a fishing pole in his hand, he reflected on his life. He was pleased with the progress he had made. It had not been easy. In fact, it had been tough. The rough times had made him appreciate everything more. He had an extra sense of pride that most others his age did not have.

Peter was 27 years old. He still had ADHD. He still took medication, and he still used his behavior and management skills. And he was happy.

Peter was engaged to be married in a month to Sabrina, the girl of his dreams. He had been asked by a successful team of optometrists to join their group. He had been with them a year and had received a letter of commendation last week. The letter had mentioned his positive attitude, his compassion for others, and the extra energy and time he put into his work. Peter knew that the tough times he had had growing up with ADHD had given him an extra sense of compassion for the people he worked with. His family also had a deep religious background. He thought that his disorder and his religion combined gave him an extra dimension in life. Still, Peter had to work hard to maintain a positive attitude. At times he still got depressed, but it was happening less often.

Peter's ADHD gave him the drive he needed to work extra hours when he was asked to. In fact, he even volunteered to work overtime. Peter needed the extra income because he and Sabrina were saving to buy a house.

Peter looked at his watch and was surprised to see how much time he had spent just sitting and thinking. He was better at relaxing than he used to be. It was time to get dressed to make the speech. His high school guidance counselor had asked him to speak to the graduating class of the small Midwestern school he had attended. She told him how proud she was of him and that the whole school considered him one of their most successful graduates. All of Peter's relatives were coming to the graduation just to hear him speak. He had spent days writing his short speech. He knew the students probably wouldn't listen, but his parents and relatives would

Peter was wrong about one thing: The students did listen. Everyone listened! Peter made a big impact. He called his speech "You Can Be a Success If You Never Give Up. The Only Disability Is Attitude!" He talked about his ADHD and how often he had failed at something and had to start again. He described how the counselor and some of his teachers and his doctor had helped him. He told the students that every one of them could be a success if they just kept trying. He encouraged them to band together to help each other. He suggested calling it an Attitude Group. He ended by reading part of the letter of commendation from his company to show how far he had come.

When he had finished, Peter was amazed to see the entire auditorium give him a standing ovation. The students, the teachers, the school administrators, the parents of the students—everyone was inspired by Peter's hard work and success.

The next week the superintendent of the school called, requesting Peter's permission to publish his speech in some of the professional journals about ADD/ADHD. To his further amazement, the school even changed some of its policies in order to identify ADD/ADHD students earlier and work with them more closely. They wanted more success stories like Peter's.

CHAPTER 9

Fantastic You

Teenagers often feel that they are branded or stamped for life because they have ADD/ADHD. They may feel they have no future because they are convinced they are dumb or stupid. They may have very low self-esteem.

You are not stupid, or lazy, or bad, or whatever else people may have said to you over the years. If you have ADD/ADHD, you have a disability. And disabilities can be overcome. We can each determine our own destiny. We can even find positive elements in ADD/ADHD. The real disability is attitude.

The Real Disability Is Attitude

One of the best predicters of success in coping with ADD/ADHD may be your attitude. Let's see how you can improve your attitude by changing negatives into positives. Coping with ADD/ADHD doesn't mean only managing the disorder. It also means adapting to it and building on your strengths.

Weakness Becomes Strength
Impatience/Impulsiveness Becomes Energy, Active-
ness
Moodiness Becomes Creativity
Easy Boredom Becomes Enthusiasm
Difficulty with Rules and Authority Becomes
Problem-Solving and Taking Control
Trouble Switching Mental Gears Becomes
Super-Focus

Impatience and Impulsiveness

If people say you are impatient and impulsive, realize that
they may be right. Rephrase it mentally; the positive side
is that you are active and energetic. Think of yourself as
an expensive, finely-tooled Ferrari racing car. You have
an accelerator, but you must also have brakes or you will
crash. It is all right for you to go fast at times, just as it is
all right for the Ferrari to go fast in appropriate places. If
it goes at 100 miles per hour on a racetrack, everyone
cheers. If it goes 100 miles per hour though a school zone,
it could crash and hurt people. The key is "appropriate
place." For example, it is not appropriate for you to tell
your teacher to "stuff it" in the middle of a classroom full
of students. But it *is* appropriate for you to tell your
teacher to "stuff it" while you are taking a shower at
home. You will be cheered if you run fast when competing
on your school's track team, but you could be in trouble if
you run at the same speed through the halls at school. It
is often not what we do but where we choose to do it that
causes our difficulties.

Notice the word *choose*. You are in control of your life,
and you make the decision whether to put on your brakes

or go full speed. Anything that runs "out of control" is dangerous.

One technique some ADD/ADHD teenagers find helpful is to visualize an imaginary speed control knob inside themselves. When it is turned to "high" or "fast," they experience everything in extremes. They get extremely impatient or impulsive, extremely upset or angry. Some things need to be done fast. ADHD teens are experts at speed.

They can also learn to turn the control knob to a slow speed when appropriate. Visualize a knob inside you. Is it in your brain? Is it in your finger? Is it in your chest? When you are in a "go slow" situation, turn your imaginary speed control down to slow. Now you can go at the appropriate speed.

Moodiness

If you are moody, can you find a creative solution to your moods? What caused your moodiness? Suppose a guy named James came up to you and called you stupid, then walked off. You would probably feel really upset. If Sue then walked up and said, "Hi," you might respond angrily to her. She would think you were moody.

Since you are in control of your life, instead of being moody with Sue you could become creative and think ahead of time of something funny to say to James the next time he called you stupid. What would James do if you responded by laughing and saying, "Well, at least I'm not rude like some people I know," and then walked off.

Then when you met Sue you would probably still be laughing, thinking of James feeling like a jerk. When Sue said, "Hi," you would be in a great mood.

Boredom

If you are easily bored, figure out what bores you. Take control of those things, and you may be able to change your attitude from boredom to enthusiasm.

For instance, you may have five pages of math homework problems to do when you want to be out with your friends. You know how to do them. They just take so long! You think it is stupid to spend so much time on something you know how to do. Take control of the situation and find a fun and creative way to do them.

For example, you might divide the task into smaller units. Fold each page in half or even fourths. Set a kitchen timer and try to "beat the clock" by finishing each section before it rings. You may save so much time that you are able to join your friends for part of the evening. If not, have another reward waiting for you when you finish. Play your favorite music or computer game if you finish before the timer goes off three out of four times. Since you are in control, you set your own reward.

Rules

If you have difficulty with rules and authority, try to figure what in particular bothers you about the rule or being told what to do. Then look for a way to make the rule more acceptable. If your mother is standing in the living room looking at the clock each night when you come in, it may not be the rule you object to. It may be the fact that your mother is checking on you. Use your creativity and come up with another solution. Maybe she could go to bed and you could come in and wake her up when you get home. If she is afraid something might happen to you and she won't know about it, she could set her alarm clock.

When you come in and awaken her, she can turn it off. If you do not show by the appointed hour, the alarm will go off and she will be aware there is a problem. Again, you're in control.

Switching Gears

Do you have trouble switching gears or get upset easily when you're interrupted? Try thinking of yourself as superfocused. ADD/ADHD students are often accused of not paying attention. They may be superfocused on something else. Use your creativity and find a way to turn this into an asset. Being superfocused can help you get one job done at a time.

Take control of the situation and figure out a cue to help you direct your "superfocus" where it needs to be. If you need to change your focus in class, for example, you might ask your teacher to walk over and lightly touch you on the shoulder when she notices you are not listening to her. You've come up with a method to keep your focus.

DARNELL

Ellen thought Darnell was one of the most handsome and popular boys in school. He was a track star. She knew Darnell had ADHD. He had confided to her that he used an imaginary inner control knob to cope with his ADHD. He needed to turn himself up for maximum speed at track, or when he got depressed. He touched his right ear to turn up his inner control knob. He touched his left ear to help himself slow down if he felt angry or impatient when it was not appropriate to show it. Darnell also turned the imaginary knob to help him relax and slow down to go to sleep at night.

Ellen had seen Darnell put his finger on his ear at times but thought nothing of it. Now she thought his creativity was one of the reasons he was so popular. He had ADHD, but he was always coming up with interesting ways to keep a positive attitude about it. Ellen thought Darnell was fantastic for coping so well.

JASON

Remember Jason, from Chapter 1? People weren't yelling at him as much anymore. In the year since he had been diagnosed with ADD, life had improved for Jason.

First his doctor had tried several medications for him. After a short time they had found the right medication at the minimum dosage he needed. His symptoms seemed more manageable right away.

Then Jason had started a program with a therapist to learn behavior management and other coping skills. His parents had also gone to the therapist, and they used their new techniques at home. Together they helped Jason work out an education plan with his teachers. He was finishing his homework now, and his grades have gone up.

The best thing was how Jason felt about himself. He had more self-confidence and he was happier. He has ADD, but he knew he could cope with it. With the help and support of people who cared about him, Jason felt that he could finally take charge of his life.

Glossary

Al-Anon Organization formed for spouses and close friends of alcoholics. It arose from Alcoholics Anonymous.

Alateen Organization formed for children of alcoholics. It arose from Alcoholics Anonymous.

Attention Deficit Disorder (ADD) Neurobiological disorder marked by habitual inability to pay attention for more than a few minutes, even when requested or punished.

Attention Deficit Hyperactivity Disorder (ADHD) Attention Deficit Disorder accompanied by extreme overactivity.

cognitive style The approach of a person to solving problems and thinking through situations.

deficit Lack or impairment of a capacity to function.

genetic Of or relating to a gene, the building block of heredity.

hereditary Transmitted from parent to offspring.

hyperactivity Excessive motor functioning or activity.

IEP (Individualized Education Plan) Comprehensive written plan for special education and all related services.

impulsivity Form of impulsive behavior in which a person acts without logically thinking through the action or situation.

multimodal Treatment of a disorder by several methods at the same time.

neurobiological Concerned with the anatomy, physiology, and pathology of the nervous system.

perception Process by which the central nervous system organizes sensory information it receives.

psychologist Person holding an advanced degree (Ph.D.) in the study of the mental or behavioral characteristics of a person or group.

Tourette's syndrome Neurological disorder characterized by involuntary behavior such as multiple neck jerks and vocal grunts, barks, and sometimes obscenities. It is named for the French neurologist Georges Gilles de la Tourette, who described it in 1885.

Appendix Medical Management of Children with Attention Deficit Disorder: Commonly Asked Questions

By
Children with Attention Deficit Disorder (CH.A.D.D)
American Academy of Child and Adolescent Psychiatry
(AACAP)
Committee of Community Psychiatry and Consultation to
Agencies of AACAP

Harvey C. Parker, Ph.D.
CH.A.D.D., Executive Director
George Storm, M.D.
CH.A.D.D., Professional Advisory Board
Theodore A. Petti, M.D., M.P.H., Chairperson
Virginia Q. Anthony, AACAP, Executive Director

1. What Is an Attention Deficit Disorder?

Attention deficit disorder (ADD), also known as attention deficit hyperactivity disorder (ADHD), is a treatable disorder which affects approximately three to five per cent of the population. Inattentiveness, impulsivity, and oftentimes, hyperactivity, are common characteristics of the disorder. Boys with ADD tend to outnumber girls by three to one, although ADD in girls is underidentified.

Some common symptoms of ADD are:

1. Excessively fidgets or squirms
2. Difficulty remaining seated
3. Easily distracted
4. Difficulty awaiting turn in games
5. Blurts out answers to questions
6. Difficulty following instructions
7. Difficulty sustaining attention
8. Shifts from one activity to another
9. Difficulty playing quietly
10. Often talks excessively
11. Often interrupts
12. Often doesn't listen to what is said
13. Often loses things
14. Often engages in dangerous activities

However, you don't have to be hyperactive to have an attention deficit disorder. In fact, up to 30 percent of children with ADD are not hyperactive at all, but still have a lot of trouble focusing attention.

2. How Can We Tell If a Child Has ADD?

Many factors can cause children to have problems paying attention besides an attention deficit disorder. Family problems, stress, discouragement, drugs, physical illness, and learning difficulties can all cause problems that look like ADD, but really aren't. To accurately identify whether a child has ADD, a comprehensive evaluation needs to be performed by professionals who are familiar with characteristics of the disorder.

> STRESS
> DISCOURAGEMENT
> PHYSICAL ILLNESS
> LEARNING DIFFICULTIES
> FAMILY PROBLEMS

The process of evaluating whether a child has ADD usually involves a variety of professionals which can include the family physician, pediatrician, child and adolescent psychiatrist or psychologist, neurologist, family counselor and teacher. Psychiatric interview, psychological and educational testing, and/or a neurological examination can provide information leading to a proper diagnosis and treatment planning. An accurate evaluation is necessary before proper treatment can begin. Complex cases in which the diagnosis is unclear or is complicated by other medical and psychiatric conditions should be seen by a physician.

Parents and teachers, being the primary sources of information about the child's ability to attend and focus at home and in school, play an integral part in the evaluation process.

3. What Kinds of Services and Programs Help Children with ADD and Their Families?

Help for the ADD child and the family is best provided through *multimodal* treatment delivered by a team of professionals who look after the medical, emotional, behavioral, and educational needs of the child. Parents play an essential role as coordinators of services and programs designed to help their child. Such services and programs may include:

- Medication to help improve attention and reduce impulsivity and hyperactivity, as well as to treat other emotional or adjustment problems which sometimes accompany ADD.
- Training parents to understand ADD and to be more effective behavior managers as well as advocates for their child.
- Counseling or training ADD children in methods of self-control, attention focusing, learning strategies, organizational skills, or social skill development.
- Psychotherapy to help the demoralized or even depressed ADD child.
- Other interventions at home and at school designed to enhance self-esteem and foster acceptance, approval, and a sense of belonging.

4. What Medications Are Prescribed for ADD Children?

Medications can dramatically improve attention span and reduce hyperactive and impulsive behavior. Psychostimulants have been used to treat attentional deficits in children since the 1940s. Antidepressants, while used less frequently to treat ADD, have been shown to be quite effective for the management of this disorder in some children.

5. How Do Psychostimulants such as Dexedrine (dextroamphetamine), Ritalin (methylphenidate) and Cylert (pemoline) Help?

Seventy to eighty per cent of ADD children respond in a positive manner to psychostimulant medication. Exactly how these medicines work is not known. However, benefits for children can be quite significant and are most apparent when concentration is required. In classroom settings, on-task behavior and completion of assigned tasks is increased, socialization with peers and teacher is improved, and disruptive behaviors (talking out, demanding attention, getting out of seat, noncompliance with requests, breaking rules) are reduced.

The specific dose of medicine must be determined for each child. Generally, the higher the dose, the greater the effect and side effects. To ensure proper dosage, regular monitoring at different levels should be done. Since there are no clear guidelines as to how long a child should take medication, periodic trials off medication should be done to determine continued need. Behavioral rating scales, testing on continuous performance tasks, and the child's self-reports provide helpful, but not infallible measures of progress.

Despite myths to the contrary, a positive response to stimulants is often found in adolescents with ADD; therefore, medication need not be discontinued as the child reaches adolescence if it is still needed.

6. What Are Common Side Effects of Psychostimulant Medications?

Reduction in appetite, loss of weight, and problems in falling asleep are the most common adverse effects. Children treated with stimulants may become irritable and more sensitive to criticism or rejection. Sadness and a tendency to cry are occasionally seen.

The unmasking or worsening of a tic disorder is an infrequent effect of stimulants. In some cases this involves Tourette's Disorder. Generally, except in Tourette's, the tics decrease or disappear with the discontinuation of the stimulant. Caution must be employed in medicating adolescents with stimulants if there are coexisting disorders, e.g. depression, substance abuse, conduct, tic or mood disorders. Likewise, caution should be employed when a family history of a tic disorder exists.

Some side effects, e.g. decreased spontaneity, are felt to be dose-related and can be alleviated by reduction of dosage or switching to another stimulant. Similarly, slowing of height and weight gain of children on stimulants has been documented, with a return to normal for both occurring upon discontinuation of the medication. Other less common side effects have been described but they may occur as frequently with a placebo as with active medication. Pemoline may cause impaired liver functioning in 3 percent of children, and this may not be completely reversed when this medication is discontinued.

Overmedication has been reported to cause impairment in cognitive functioning and alertness. Some children on higher doses of stimulants will experience what has been described as a "rebound" effect, consisting of changes in mood, irritability and increases of the symptoms associated with their disorder. This occurs with variable degrees of severity during the late afternoon or evening, when the level of medicine in the blood falls. Thus, an additional low dose of medicine in the late afternoon or a decrease of the noontime dose might be required.

7. When Are Tricyclic Antidepressants Such as Tofranil (imipramine), Norpramin (desipramine) and Elavil (amytriptyline) Used to Treat ADD Children?

This group of medications is generally considered when contraindications to stimulants exist, when stimulants have not been effective or have resulted in unacceptable side effects, or when the antidepressant property is more critical to treatment than the decrease of inattentiveness. They are used much less frequently than the stimulants, seem to have a different mechanism of action, and may be somewhat less effective than the psychostimulants in treating ADD. Long-term use of the tricyclics has not been well studied. Children with ADD who are also experiencing anxiety or depression may do best with an initial trial of a tricyclic antidepressant followed, if needed, with a stimulant for the more classic ADD symptoms.

8. What Are the Side Effects of Tricyclic Antidepressant Medications?

Side effects include constipation and dry mouth. Symptomatic treatment with stool softeners and sugarfree gum or candy are usually effective in alleviating the discomfort. Confusion, elevated blood pressure, possible precipitation of manic-like behavior and inducement of seizures are uncommon side effects. The latter three occur in vulnerable individuals who can generally be identified during the assessment phase.

9. What About ADD Children Who Do Not Respond Well to Medication?

Some ADD children or adolescents will not respond satisfactorily to either the psychostimulant or tricyclic antidepressant medications. Non-responders may have severe symptoms of ADD, may have other problems in addition to ADD, or may not be able to tolerate certain medications due to adverse side effects as noted above. In such cases consultation with a child and adolescent psychiatrist may be helpful.

10. How Often Should Medications Be Dispensed at School to an ADD Child?

Since the duration for effective action for Ritalin and Dexedrine, the most commonly used psychostimulants, is only about four hours, a second dose during school is often required. Taking a second dose of medication at noontime enables the ADD child to focus attention effectively, utilize appropriate school behavior and maintain academic productivity. However, the noontime dose can sometimes be eliminated for children whose afternoon academic schedule does not require high levels of attentiveness. Some psychostimulants, i.e. SR Ritalin (sustained release form) and Cylert, work for longer periods of time (eight to ten hours) and may help avoid the need for a noontime dose. Antidepressant medications used to treat ADD are usually taken in the morning, afternoon hours after school, or in the evening.

In many cases the physician may recommend that medication be continued at non-school times such as weekday afternoons, weekends or school vacations. During such non-school times lower doses of medication than those taken for school may be sufficient. It is important to remember that ADD is more than a school problem—it is a problem which often interferes in the learning of constructive social, peer, and sports activities.

11. How Should Medication Be Dispensed at School

Most important, regardless of who dispenses medication, since an ADD child may already feel "different" from others, care should be taken to provide discreet reminders to the child when it is time to take medication. It is quite important that school personnel treat the administration of medication in a sensitive manner, thereby safeguarding the privacy of the child or adolescent and avoiding any unnecessary embarrassment. Success in doing this will increase the student's compliance in taking medication.

The location for dispensing medication at school may vary depending upon the school's resources. In those schools with a full-time nurse, the infirmary would be the first choice. In those schools in which a nurse is not always available, other properly trained school personnel may take the responsibility of supervising and dispensing medication.

12. How Should the Effectiveness of Medication and Other Treatments for the ADD Child Be Monitored?

Important information needed to judge the effectiveness of medication usually comes from reports by the child's parents and teachers and should include information about the child's behavior and attentiveness, academic performance, social and emotional adjustment and any medication side effects.

Reporting from these sources may be informal through telephone, or more objective via the completion of scales designed for this purpose.

The commonly used teacher rating scales are:

- Conners Teacher Rating Scales
- ADD-H Comprehensive Teacher Rating Scale
- Child Behavior Checklist
- ADHD Rating Scale
- Child Attention Problems (CAP) Rating Scale
- School Situations Questionnaire

Academic performance should be monitored by comparing classroom grades prior to and after treatment.

It is important to monitor changes in peer relationships, family functioning, social skills, a capacity to enjoy leisure time, and self-esteem.

The parents, school nurse, or other school personnel responsible for dispensing or overseeing the medication trial should have regular contact by phone with the prescribing physician. Physician office visits of sufficient frequency to monitor treatment are critical in the overall care of children with ADD.

13. What Is the Role of the Teacher in the Care of Children with ADD?

Teaching an ADD child can test the limits of any educator's time and patience. As any parent of an ADD child will tell you, being on the front lines helping these children to manage on a daily basis can be both challenging and exhausting. It helps if teachers know what to expect and if they receive in-service training on how to teach and manage ADD students in their classroom.

Here are some ideas that teachers told us have helped:

- Build upon the child's strengths by offering a great deal of encouragement and praise for the child's efforts, no matter how small.
- Learn to use behavior modification programs that motivate students to focus attention, behave better, and complete work.
- Talk with the child's parents and find helpful strategies that have worked with the child in the past.
- If the child is taking medication, communicate frequently with the physician (and parents) so that proper adjustments can be made with respect to type or dose of medication. Behavior rating scales are good for this purpose.
- Modify the classroom structure to accommodate the child's span of attention, i.e. shorter assignments, preferential seating in the classroom, appealing curriculum material, animated presentation of lessons, and frequent positive reinforcement.
- Determine whether the child can be helped through special educational resources within the school.
- Consult with other school personnel such as the guidance counselor, school psychologist, or school nurse to get their ideas as well.

14. What Are Common Myths Associated with ADD Medications?

Myth: Medication should be stopped when a child reaches teen years.

Fact: Research clearly shows that there is continued benefit to medication for those teens who meet criteria for diagnosis of ADD.

Myth: Children build up a tolerance of medication.

Fact: Although the dose of medication may need adjusting from time to time, there is no evidence that children build up a tolerance to medication.

Myth: Taking medication for ADD leads to greater likelihood of later drug addiction.

Fact: There is no evidence to indicate that ADD medication leads to an increased likelihood of later drug addiction.

Myth: Positive response to medication is confirmation of a diagnosis of ADD.

Fact: The fact that a child shows improvement of attention span or a reduction of activity while taking ADD medication does not substantiate the diagnosis of ADD. Even some normal children will show a marked improvement in attentiveness when they take ADD medications.

Myth: Medication stunts growth.

Fact: ADD medications may cause an initial and mild slowing of growth, but over time the growth suppression effect is minimal if non-existent in most cases.

Myth: Taking ADD medications as a child makes you more reliant on drugs as an adult.

Fact: There is no evidence of increased medication taking when medicated ADD children become adults, nor is there evidence that ADD children become addicted to their medications.

Myth: ADD children who take medication attribute their success only to medication.

Fact: When self-esteem is encouraged, a child taking medication attributes his success not only to the medication but to himself as well.

Summary of Important Points

1. ADD children make up 3–5% of the population. but many children who have trouble paying attention may have problems other than ADD. A thorough evaluation can help determine whether attentional deficits are due to ADD or to other conditions.
2. Once identified, ADD children are best treated with a multimodal approach. Best results are obtained when

behavioral management programs, educational interventions, parent training, counseling, and medication, when needed, are used together to help the ADD child. Parents of children and adolescents with ADD play the key role of coordinating these services.

3. Each ADD child responds in his or her own unique way to medication depending upon the child's physical make-up, severity of ADD symptoms, and other possible problems accompanying the ADD. Responses to medication need to be monitored and reported to the child's physician.

4. Teachers play an essential role in helping the ADD child feel comfortable within the classroom procedures, and work demands, sensitivity to self-esteem issues, and frequent parent-teacher contact can help a great deal.

5. ADD may be a lifelong disorder requiring lifelong assistance. Families, and the children themselves, need our continued support and understanding.

6. Successful treatment of the medical aspects of ADD is dependent upon ongoing collaboration between the prescribing physician, teacher, therapist, and parents.

Help List

Most states in the United States have organizations devoted to providing information and assistance in the areas of Attention Deficit Disorder, Attention Deficit Hyperactivity Disorder, and various learning disabilities. Consult your local telephone directory, or write for information to the following national organizations:

UNITED STATES

Attention Deficit Disorders Association (ADDA)
4300 West Park Boulevard
Plano, TX 75093

Children and Adults with Attention Deficit Disorder
   (CH.A.D.D.)
499 Northwest 70th Avenue
Plantation, FL 33317
(305) 587-3700

Learning Disabilities Association of America
4156 Library Road
Pittsburgh, PA 15234
(412) 341-1515

National Attention Deficit Disorders Association (ADDA)
8091 South Ireland Way
Aurora, CO 80016
(800) 487-2282

CANADA

Learning Disabilities Association of Canada
200, 323 Chapel Street
Ottawa, DN KIN 772
(613) 238-5721

Learning Disabilities Research and Information c/o Department
    of Education
P.O. Box 578
Halifax, NS B3J 259
(902) 424 4823

For Further Reading

Barkley, R. *Defiant Children*. New York: Guilford Press, 1987.

Clayton, Lawrence, and Morrison, J. *Coping with Learning Disability*. New York: Rosen Publishing Group, 1992.

Fowler, M.D. *Maybe You Know My Child*. New York: Birch Lane Press, 1990.

Friedman, R., and Doyal, G.T. *The Hyperactive Child*. St. Clair Shores: Educational Resources Clinic.

Gordon, M. *I Would If I Could: A Teenager's Guide to ADHD*. Syracuse: GST Press, 1993.

———. *Jumpin' Johnny: Get Back to Work*. Syracuse: GSI Press, 1991.

———. *My Brother's a World-Class Pain: A Sibling's Guide to ADHD*. Syracuse: GSI Press, 1991.

———. *ADHD/Hyperactivity: A Consumer's Guide*. Syracuse: GSI Publications, 1990.

Greenberg, G.S., and Horn, W.F. *ADHD: Questions and Answers for Parents*. Champaign, IL: Research Press, 1991.

Hallowell, Dr. Edward M., and Ratey, Dr. John R. *Driven to Distraction: Recognizing and Coping with Attention Deficit Disorder from Childhood through Adulthood*. New York: Pantheon, 1994.

Ingersoll. B. *Your Hyperactive Child*. New York: Doubleday, 1988.

Kelly, K., and Ramundo, P. *You Mean I'm Not Lazy, Stupid, or Crazy: A Self-Help Book for Adults with Attention Deficit Disorders*. Cincinnati: Tyrell & Jerem Press, 1993.

Nadeau, K., and Dixon, E. *Learning to Slow Down and Pay Attention*. Chesapeake Psychological Services, 1991.

Packer, A. *Bringing Up Parents: The Teenager's Handbook*.

Minneapolis: Free Spirit Publishing, 1992.

Parker, R.N. *Making the Grade: An Adolescent's Struggle with ADD*. Plantation, FL: Impact Publications, 1992.

Phelan, T.W. *All About Attention Deficit: Symptoms, Diagnosis, and Treatment: Children and Adults*. Glen Ellyn, IL: Child Management Inc., 1993.

Quinn, P.O., and Stern, J.M. *Putting on the Brakes*. New York: Magination Press, 1991.

Index